Reading Essentials®
in Social Studies

U.S. REGIONAL ROAD TRIP

The Southeast

MARTHA SIAS PURCELL

PERFECTION LEARNING®

Editorial Director: Susan C. Thies
Editor: Mary L. Bush
Design Director: Randy Messer
Book Design: Jennifer Beaman, Emily J. Greazel
Cover Design: Michael A. Aspengren

Image Credits:
© Jim McDonald/CORBIS: p. 9 (top right); © Kevin Fleming/CORBIS: p. 20;
© Buddy Mays/CORBIS: pp. 8, 27 (top); © Phil Schermeister/CORBIS: p. 29 (bottom);
© Bettmann/CORBIS: pp. 32, 35; © CORBIS: p. 33 (bottom); © Reuters/CORBIS: p. 34

ClipArt.com: pp. 10, 11, 13 (left), 15, 22; Photos.com: cover, pp. 1, 2 (top and bottom),
3 (bottom left), 4 (background), 6, 7, 9 (background and top left), 10 (background), 12,
16, 19 (background), 22 (background), 23, 24, 25, 26 (background), 29 (top),
32 (background), 36–37, 38–39, 40; digitalSTOCK: p. 9 (bottom); © Louisiana Office
of Tourism: pp. 21, 33 (top); Dan Brothers/Alabama Bureau of Tourism & Travel: p. 31;
Courtesy of Kentuckytourism.com: p. 30 (left); Courtesy of the Georgia Department of
Industry, Trade & Tourism: p. 19; Courtesy of NC Division of Tourism, Film, and Sports
Development: pp. 3 (top), 27 (bottom); Courtesy of the Mississippi Development
Authority/Division of Tourism: p. 3 (middle); Courtesy of the Arkansas Department of
Parks and Tourism: pp. 2 (middle), 30 (right); Douglas Peebles/Virginia Tourism
Corporation: p. 28 (top); West Virginia Division of Tourism: p. 28 (bottom);
MapResources: pp. 3 (bottom right), 4 (map), 5, 13 (right), 14; Library of Congress:
p. 18

For information, contact
Perfection Learning® Corporation
1000 North Second Avenue, P.O. Box 500
Logan, Iowa 51546-0500.
Phone: 1-800-831-4190
Fax: 1-800-543-2745
perfectionlearning.com

1 2 3 4 5 6 PP 09 08 07 06 05 04

ISBN 0-7891-6322-5

Table of Contents

Chapter 1

Introducing the Southeast

L arge trees dripping with gray moss surround cotton plantations. Banjo tunes echo from a cruising riverboat. Families gather around tables piled with fried chicken, biscuits, and watermelon. These are the sights, sounds, and tastes of the Southeast. Alabama, Arkansas, Florida, Georgia, Kentucky, Louisiana, Mississippi, North Carolina, South Carolina, Tennessee, Virginia, and West Virginia form this 528,700-square-mile region of the United States.

Also Known As . . .

The Southeast is also known as the South.

The Land

Millions of years ago, huge sheets of ice covered the upper half of the Southeast. Seawater covered the rest. Near the center of the region, a chain of mountains was thrust up from deep within the earth.

Today, the glaciers have melted and the seawater has dried up or **receded**. **Plateaus**, **plains**, and coastal lowlands remain. The Appalachian Mountain chain divides the region into two areas of land with distinct features.

The Appalachian Plateau lies to the west of the mountains. These flat highlands reach across the western edge of the Southeast. Then they gradually slope downward into the central plains of the Midwest.

The Appalachians stretch from Canada to Alabama. These mountains are some of the oldest in the world. At one time, they stood tall at nearly 20,000 feet. But today, the Appalachians are no longer steep and rugged. Over millions of years, water and weather have worn them down. The Allegheny Mountains, Blue Ridge Mountains, and Great Smoky Mountains are several smaller southeastern ranges within the Appalachian chain. These mountains are covered with forests and grasslands.

- Allegheny Mountains
- Great Smoky Mountains
- Blue Ridge Mountains

The Piedmont begins at the eastern base of the Appalachian Mountains. These rolling hills of rich farmland rest between the mountains and the Atlantic Coastal Plain. The eastern edge of the Piedmont is called the Fall Line. River waterfalls and white-water rapids rush down this sudden drop to the coastal plains.

The Atlantic Coastal Plain stretches from Virginia to Florida. This plain is laced with inlets, bays, and coves. **Barrier islands** lining the coast protect the mainland from **erosion**.

The Florida Keys are a chain of small islands that trail west from the southern tip of Florida. A single highway with 42 bridges connects these many islands.

The Gulf of Mexico shapes the lower edge of the Southeast. Bayous, swamps, and salt domes are found along the southern coast.

Water Words

- A bay is an area of sea enclosed by a stretch of curved coastline.

- A bayou is an area of slow-moving water leading from a river or lake.

- A cove is a small bay on the shore of a sea that is often enclosed by high cliffs.

- An inlet is a narrow stretch of water reaching toward the mainland from the sea.

- A salt dome is a dome-shaped structure formed when buried salt pushes up through rock layers.

- A swamp is an area of land that is always wet and usually overgrown with trees and other plants.

Aerial view of the Gulf of Mexico

The Southeast has several large cave systems. Mammoth Cave in Kentucky, Blanchard Springs Caverns in Arkansas, Russell Cave in Alabama, and Luray Caverns in Virginia are just a few of the caves found across the region. These caves, or caverns, were formed when rainwater dissolved limestone rock, carving out large and small spaces.

The Water

Many rivers flow through the Southeast. The Cumberland, Savannah, Arkansas, Tennessee, Alabama, Red, and Roanoke Rivers wind through the region. The Ohio River forms the northern borders of Kentucky and West Virginia.

The Mississippi River runs along the western borders of Kentucky, Tennessee, and Mississippi. The **alluvial plain** beside the river is prime farmland. When the river meets the Gulf of Mexico, it deposits the **silt** it's been carrying. This creates an area of **fertile** soil called the Mississippi Delta.

Delta Details

A delta is a triangular deposit of silt (sand and soil) at the mouth of a river. The mouth is the place where the river enters a sea or lake.

The Southeast has only a few natural lakes. The largest one is Lake Okeechobee in Florida. **Dams** built across rivers in the region have created many artificial lakes as well.

The Everglades is a national park covering the southern tip of Florida. This **subtropical** "river of grass" has both freshwater and saltwater environments. Many species of animals live among the saw grass and towering cypress and mangrove trees.

Everglades

Another major **wetland** in the Southeast is the Okefenokee National Wildlife Refuge in southern Georgia and northern Florida. *Okefenokee* means "land of the trembling Earth." The Okefenokee Swamp has thick **peat deposits** on its floor. These unsteady deposits sometimes cause trees and bushes to tremble when people stomp on the swamp's surface. **Decaying** plants in the swamp make the water look like brown tea.

The Climate

The Southeast has mild winters and hot summers. January temperatures in the region average from 30°F to more than 60°F. July temperatures average from 75° to 90°F. The northern states and mountain areas in the region are slightly cooler. The southern half can be very hot, with high humidity making conditions steamy.

The Southeast has more **precipitation** than most of the United States. The region receives 40 to 75+ inches of precipitation a year, mostly in the form of rainfall. Snow does fall in the northern states and the mountains, and ice storms can occur in the southern states.

Healing Waters

The Southeast is also known for its warm mineral waters. Some people believe these natural **springs** have healing powers. The springs were especially popular before the discovery of antibiotics. Many people came hoping to cure illnesses or diseases.

Hot Springs National Park, Arkansas

Hurricanes that begin in the Caribbean Sea and Atlantic Ocean sometimes rip through the Southeast. These storms of wind, rain, and waves leave wide paths of death and destruction. Southern Florida, from Cape Canaveral to the Florida Keys, is referred to as "Hurricane Alley." Hurricanes often hit this stretch of the coast. They also slam into the Gulf Coast states of Louisiana, Mississippi, and Alabama. The National Hurricane Center is located in Coral Gables, Florida.

The Southeast also experiences tornadoes. These swirling funnel clouds twist through many southeastern states during the spring and summer months. Alabama, Arkansas, Florida, Georgia, Louisiana, and Mississippi are the southeastern states most at risk for tornadoes.

Chapter 2

Exploring the Southeast

The Fountain of Youth

Most Spanish explorers wanted one thing—gold! However, the first Spaniard in the Southeast was searching for something else. Juan Ponce de León wanted to drink from the Fountain of Youth so he wouldn't grow old. Unfortunately, this fountain was just a legend, and Ponce de León left Florida in disappointment. He did, however, tell another Spanish explorer about the **New World**.

Florida's Feast of Flowers

Ponce de León arrived on the southeastern coast during the Easter season, or *Pascua Florida* in Spain. Because of this and the magnificent magnolia trees full of flowers (*florida*), he called the land "Pascua de Florida," which later became Florida.

Golden Dreams

Hernando de Soto's only interest was gold. When Ponce de León told him about the New World, de Soto decided to go there in search of the precious metal.

De Soto and his men landed on the western coast of Florida in 1540 and began a journey that would last almost four years. In addition to Florida, they traveled through what later became Georgia, South Carolina, Alabama, Tennessee, Mississippi, Louisiana, and Arkansas.

Miles of soft white sand and tall grasses greeted the explorers. Mangrove trees grew with twisted branches and upturned roots. De Soto stood under towering cypress trees in steamy swamps. Insect-eating plants, like the Venus flytrap and the pitcher plant, fascinated him. On more solid ground, he rested in the shade of oak trees with widespread branches.

Spanish moss hung from these branches like unruly gray-green beards.

As de Soto moved toward the Appalachian Mountains, the plant life changed. Pines, maples, and other hardwoods covered the hills. Bright blooms of azaleas, magnolias, dogwood, and rhododendrons splashed across the landscape.

The explorers had to watch for alligators and poisonous snakes in the swampy areas. In the mountains, they were more likely to see deer, black bears, raccoons, and foxes.

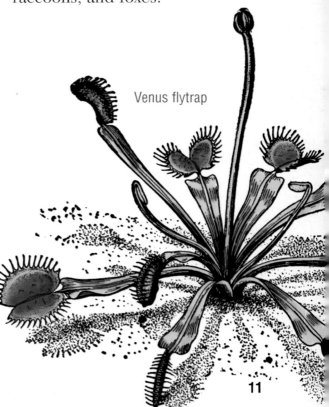

Venus flytrap

De Soto was the first European to see the Mississippi River. Unfortunately, it became his place of burial when he became ill and died in Alabama. He never did find gold in the New World. Centuries later, however, this valuable metal was discovered in Georgia and North Carolina.

Settling the Southeast

Half of de Soto's men died on the journey, but the survivors told their friends in Spain about the beautiful lands they'd seen. In 1565, Spanish **colonists** established St. Augustine, Florida, as the first permanent European settlement in the United States.

An English colony was founded in 1587 on Roanoke Island off the coast of North Carolina. When other colonists arrived from England three years later, the islanders had vanished! They were never found, and the mystery of the missing colonists was never solved.

Other colonists continued to arrive in the New World. In 1607, Jamestown, Virginia, became the first permanent English colony in the Southeast. Spain and France eventually settled areas of Florida, Louisiana, Arkansas, and Mississippi.

Dangerous Waters

During the 1600s and 1700s, sailing along the Atlantic Coast and the Gulf of Mexico could be dangerous. Pirates like Blackbeard, Captain Kidd, and Jean Lafitte captured ships going to and from the colonies. Stories tell of pirates' treasures buried off the southeastern coast.

Slavery Comes to the New World

Native Americans taught the colonists how to raise crops, such as tobacco, cotton, **indigo**, and rice. But harvesting large quantities of these crops was hard work. More workers were needed.

As early as 1619, Africans were kidnapped and shipped to

the New World to be sold as slaves. Slavery became big business in the Southeast. Alabama, Louisiana, South Carolina, and Virginia had major slave-trading seaports.

Average plantations had up to 25 slaves, but the largest kept hundreds of African Americans. Slaves served as carpenters, blacksmiths, field hands, and house servants.

A New Nation

In 1776, the thirteen original colonies, including Georgia, North Carolina, South Carolina, and Virginia, were tired of paying unfair taxes to the king of England. The colonies declared their independence, won the American Revolutionary War, and became the United States of America.

What Were the Other Original Colonies?

Besides Georgia, North Carolina, South Carolina, and Virginia, the other nine original colonies were Connecticut, Delaware, Maryland, Massachusetts, New Hampshire, New Jersey, New York, Pennsylvania, and Rhode Island.

New Hampshire
New York
Connecticut
Rhode Island
Massachusetts
Pennsylvania
New Jersey
Delaware
Maryland
Virginia
North Carolina
South Carolina
Georgia

"Going out west" in the early 1700s meant making the difficult trip to the other side of the Appalachian Mountains. People generally avoided the mountains and traveled on the Ohio River to the Mississippi River instead.

Then in 1750, an explorer named Thomas Walker discovered the Cumberland Gap. This natural passageway formed where Tennessee, Kentucky, and Virginia meet. In the later 1700s, pioneers streamed through the Cumberland Gap and settled the remaining areas of the Southeast.

Statehood

Georgia, South Carolina, and Virginia became the first southeastern states in 1788. North Carolina followed in 1789. Kentucky became a state on June 1, 1792. Tennessee was admitted to the Union in 1796. Louisiana became a state in 1812, followed by Mississippi in 1817, Alabama in 1819, and Arkansas in 1836. Florida joined the Union in 1845. West Virginia became a state in 1863, when it broke away from Virginia.

Moving the Native Americans

Native Americans gradually lost their land to the settlers. Bloody battles were fought, and treaties were signed. But settlers kept coming, and treaties were broken. In 1830, the federal government ordered all Native Americans to "Indian Territory," which later became the state of Oklahoma.

A few tribes moved as ordered, but most stayed to fight

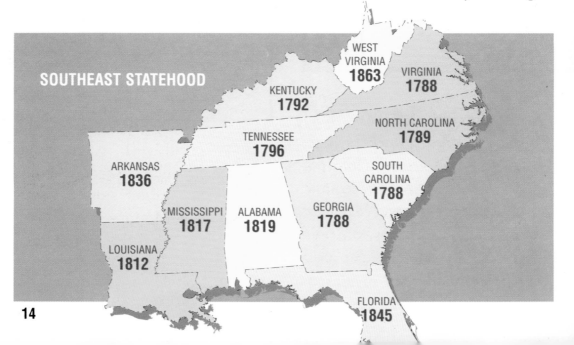

SOUTHEAST STATEHOOD

WEST VIRGINIA 1863

VIRGINIA 1788

KENTUCKY 1792

NORTH CAROLINA 1789

TENNESSEE 1796

ARKANSAS 1836

SOUTH CAROLINA 1788

MISSISSIPPI 1817

ALABAMA 1819

GEORGIA 1788

LOUISIANA 1812

FLORIDA 1845

for their land. The Seminoles of Florida fought three wars. The last one ended in 1858. Only several hundred Seminoles remained by this time, and they retreated to the Everglades. The Cherokees, who lived like Europeans, tried to fight through the court system. But by 1838, they, too, were forced to leave. Thousands of Cherokee died on the walk from Georgia to Oklahoma. Their journey became known as the "Trail of Tears."

Slavery Grows

The slave population in the South continued to grow. Sometimes slaves outnumbered the white population. Plantation owners took action to make sure that the huge number of slaves didn't **revolt**.

Rules were set for slaves. If they disobeyed these rules, they were punished—often severely. Slaves were not allowed to read or write. Slaves couldn't worship in their own way but had to sit in the balcony of their masters' churches. The few who could leave the plantation needed a pass from their owner.

The use of slaves was the basis of the Southeast's **economy**. Not all southerners agreed with slavery. Still, most believed that the individual states—not the federal government—should make their own decisions about slavery.

In the meantime, the Northeast region of the United States had an economy based on industry. Most northeasterners disagreed strongly with the practice of slavery. Eventually the issue of slavery would tear the country apart.

The Civil War

Abraham Lincoln was elected president in 1860. Shortly after, South Carolina seceded, or withdrew, from the Union. Its citizens wanted to create their own country with laws that would protect slavery.

The Union

Before the Civil War, the phrase "the Union" referred to the entire United States of America. At the time of the war, it came to stand for the northern states that fought against slavery.

On January 9, 1861, Mississippi joined South Carolina. A few months later, 11 states had formed the Confederate States of America, or the Confederacy. The Confederacy included Florida, Mississippi, Alabama, Georgia, Louisiana, Texas, Virginia, Arkansas, Tennessee, North Carolina, and South Carolina. Jefferson Davis was elected president of the Confederacy, and the capital was established in Richmond, Virginia.

Kentucky, Maryland, and Tennessee were on the border between the Confederacy and the Union. These states had difficulty deciding which side to join. In the end, Kentucky and Maryland stayed with the Union, while Tennessee joined the Confederacy. People in the western third of Virginia were against slavery. In 1863, they decided to break away and form West Virginia, a new state that remained in the Union.

The Civil War began on April 12, 1861, with shots fired at Fort Sumter off the coast of South Carolina. The next four years were a sad chapter in United States history. Brothers fought brothers. Fathers fought sons. Farms were destroyed, and

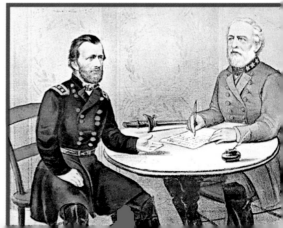

In April of 1865, Confederate General Robert E. Lee surrendered to Union General Ulysses S. Grant at Appomattox Court House in Virginia.

entire cities were looted and burned by fellow countrymen. In April of 1865, the Confederacy was forced to surrender. The North had won, and slavery would come to an end.

After the War

After the war, both the economy and the land in the Southeast were ruined. Newly freed slaves roamed the region, not knowing where to go. Some became **sharecroppers** for their former masters. The plantation owners paid the workers very little and charged high rent for shacks and high prices for supplies. Soon the freed slaves were in debt. Once again, the owners were in control.

Amendments 13, 14, and 15 of the Constitution are a result of the Civil War. The 13th Amendment forbids slavery. The 14th Amendment says that anyone born in the United States is a citizen with equal rights protected by law. The 15th Amendment gives all male citizens the right to vote.

The Confederate states had to agree to these amendments before they were readmitted to the Union. However, the states found ways to get around the rights promised to African Americans. They carefully—and even legally—made **segregation** a way of life in the South.

Each state passed "Black Codes" that kept the newly freed slaves from exercising their rights. For example, African Americans could vote, but they had to prove they were educated. Since it had been against the law to educate slaves, few African Americans in the Southeast knew how to read and write.

"Jim Crow Laws" were also created to segregate African Americans. These laws allowed "separate but equal" facilities. Schools, drinking fountains, restrooms, and waiting rooms were set aside "for coloreds only." But most of these places were "less equal" than those of the white people.

Civil Rights

In 1954, the Supreme Court ruled against "separate but equal" laws. Some southern states resisted change. For example, sometimes U.S. troops were needed to help **integrate** schools so all races could attend. The soldiers protected African American students who were sent to schools with white students.

Martin Luther King, Jr., a pastor from Montgomery, Alabama, tried to promote change through nonviolent demonstrations and marches. He told protestors not to fight back.

Sometimes King's followers were jailed and even killed. Dr. King himself was **assassinated** in 1968, but not before he left a tremendous mark on the road to equality for African Americans.

News stories told the entire country about the living conditions of southern African Americans. The region was pressured to **reform**. One by one, laws were enforced and improvements were made. Life in the Southeast was forever changed.

The New South

Today, the history of the region is often divided into the "Old South" and the "New South." The Old South was the time before the Civil War, when plantations were plentiful and slavery was a way of life. The New South is a region of more freedom and equality for all its people. It is a more industrial area that doesn't rely as heavily on agriculture. However, the traditional "southern **hospitality** and charm" of the Old South can still be found among modern life in the New South.

Chapter 3

Southeastern People
Past and Present

Southerners are proud of their cultural roots. Many integrate the traditions of the Old South into their modern lives.

Native Americans

Thousands of years ago, Native American ancestors entered North America by way of an ancient land bridge that joined Russia and Alaska. From 800 to 1500 A.D., Mound Builders lived along the Mississippi River. Many of their **mounds** still exist today. Some can be found in Etowah Indian Mounds State Park in Georgia. Although there is no written history, scientists believe these people had an advanced culture of trade, craftsmanship, and religion.

Etowah Indian Mounds

When Europeans started settling in the Southeast, five main Native American tribes lived in the region—the Creeks, Cherokees, Choctaws, Seminoles, and Chickasaws. These tribes were called the "Five Civilized Tribes" because they lived like the white settlers. Many Native Americans died from European diseases or were driven off their land by settlers. A few remain in the region today and share their heritage through dance, crafts, and storytelling.

Cherokee dancers perform at the Chehaw National Indian Festival in Georgia.

Immigrants and Slaves

Various cultures have influenced the Southeast. Early **immigrants** to the region were English, Spanish, French, Irish, Scottish, Italian, and German. In recent years, Florida has seen a large growth in its Latin American population.

Many of the European immigrants settled in the southern Appalachians. When coal mines closed in the mid-1900s, thousands of people lost their jobs. The area suffered. Education, medicines, and supplies were scarce. The people of this remote mountain area lived in extreme poverty until the 1960s when the government began providing support. The Appalachian people are known for their rich traditions of music, crafts, and folktales.

After the end of slavery, many African Americans stayed in the Southeast. A high percentage of African Americans still live in the region today.

Plantations on the islands off North Carolina, South Carolina, and Georgia could only be reached by water. Their slaves were forbidden to leave, so they formed their own society with its own language. Gullah blends English vocabulary with African grammar and pronunciation. The Gullah culture reflects the African homeland of the people through traditional music, crafts, and foods. Today, the Gullah culture still flourishes on these islands.

Creoles and Cajuns

Creoles are **descendants** of wealthy French and Spanish settlers and free blacks from the West Indies. The Creoles were considered an upper class in Louisiana and Georgia.

Another group, the Acadians, left France for religious reasons. About 3000 Acadians settled in southern Louisiana. In time, their name was shortened to "Cajuns."

The Creoles treated the Cajuns as a lower class. The Cajuns withdrew to the swamps of Louisiana and lived by themselves for many years. Today, both groups add their unique style and flavor to the Southeast.

Musical Notes

Zydeco is a kind of music made famous by the Creoles and Cajuns. Violins, guitars, and accordions are the main instruments for these lively tunes. Scraping the rippled metal of a washboard creates rhythms for the songs.

Today's Population

Approximately 72 million people live in the Southeast. Almost half of the people in the region live in **rural** areas. Alabama and Florida are the only two states that have a high **urban** population of 85 percent and above. Florida is the fifth largest state in the nation with a population of about 17 million. The three largest cities in region are Atlanta, Georgia; Memphis, Tennessee; and Jacksonville, Florida.

Chapter 4

Resources
and Industries
in the Region

The Southeast has always made good use of its **natural resources**. In the past, the economy of the region was based primarily on agriculture, but more recently, industry has steadily increased in importance.

Agriculture

The phrase "cotton is king" has described southeastern agriculture since the 1700s. In the beginning, separating the seeds from the puffy white cotton bolls by hand was a slow and painful task. In 1793, Eli Whitney invented the cotton gin to do this work. This time-saver made it possible to plant and produce more cotton.

In the 1920s, swarms of beetles called *boll weevils* sucked the life out of the cotton crop and crippled the economy of the Southeast. Some farmers began growing tobacco and rice, which became other important southeastern crops. The harvesting of peanuts, pecans, and other nuts also boosted the economy.

The long growing season in the Southeast is perfect for many crops. Peaches and watermelons thrive, along with citrus fruits like oranges, grapefruits, and limes. In the 1940s, a way to make frozen orange juice concentrate was developed in Florida. Even more oranges were grown to meet the demand.

Fields of Blue-Green

Horse breeding and racing have deep roots in the Southeast, especially Kentucky. Miles of white fence surround the many horse-breeding farms in the region. The bluegrass of Kentucky is good grazing land for thoroughbred horses. The Kentucky Derby, which began in 1875, is the oldest annual horserace in the United States.

Rock and Mineral Resources

Coal is a major southeastern resource, particularly in West Virginia and Kentucky. Strip-mining is used to remove this fuel from the ground. Layers of soil are dug out to expose the coal.

Off-shore drilling makes Louisiana a major supplier of oil, natural gas, and petroleum products. The state is a large source of salt as well.

23

Various types of stone are produced in the Southeast. Limestone is found near the region's many rivers. Gemstones, like rubies, have been discovered in North Carolina.

Granite and marble are southeastern rocks. They are used for countertops, flooring, and statues. One of the region's most popular tourist sites is on the face of a granite mountain in Georgia. Stone Mountain has a gigantic carving of three Southern heroes—Jefferson Davis, Robert E. Lee, and Andrew Jackson. Much of the Lincoln Memorial in Washington, D.C., is made of marble from the Southeast. The floor is Tennessee pink marble, and the ceiling is Alabama marble. The statue of Lincoln is white Georgia marble, while the statue's base is Tennessee marble.

Industries

Many of the Southeast's raw materials supply its factories. For example, forests become wood and paper products, while cotton is made into **textiles**. Poultry and beef processing plants depend on chicken and cattle production.

Shipbuilding has been a key industry in the Southeast for hundreds of years. Warships are built in the region's factories. During peacetime, **merchant** vessels and passenger ships are constructed.

The U.S. military employs many southeasterners. The mild climate and ocean waters make the region a good place to establish bases and ports. NASA, the National Aeronautics and Space Administration, has various facilities throughout the Southeast. U.S. space missions

are launched from John F. Kennedy Space Center in Florida.

Waterways in the Southeast have always been busy. **Barges** move goods up and down rivers, especially the Mississippi. Seaports like Norfolk, Virginia, and New Orleans, Louisiana, are main gateways for travel and shipping across the Atlantic.

Fishing and Aquaculture

With so much seacoast surrounding the Southeast, it's not surprising that seafood is a major product in the region.

Shrimp is a primary catch, along with oysters, fish, and other ocean creatures.

In addition to fishing, a booming **aquaculture** business contributes to the area's economy. Large quantities of fish and shellfish are raised on farms. These farms are rivers, lakes, or other bodies of water where people control the conditions so fish can multiply quickly. Mississippi is known for its catfish farms. The catfish are then used to supply restaurants or stock recreational fishing waters.

People and Money Flock to Florida

The mild climate, miles of coastline, and long list of attractions bring many people to Florida. Some are tourists who spend a week or two seeing the sights like Disneyland, Sea World, and Busch Gardens. Others spend the entire winter there to escape from harsh weather in other states. These visitors and part-time residents significantly boost the Southeast's economy with their spending.

Chapter 5

Main Attractions in the Southeast

Each region in the United States has its own unique attractions. Let's take a brief tour of a few of these special spots in the Southeast.

American Museum of Science and Energy

The American Museum of Science and Energy in Oak Ridge, Tennessee, was originally an atomic bomb laboratory during World War II. The story of the lab is explained, but peaceful uses for atomic energy are also displayed. Self-directed science activities allow visitors to explore light, sound, static electricity, robotics, and other areas of interest.

Boone Hall Plantation and Gardens

What was the South like before the Civil War? A walk into the past at this working plantation near Mt. Pleasant, South Carolina, will help answer that question. Established in 1681, the plantation today includes 9 of the original 27 slave cabins as well as other buildings like the Cotton Gin House and the Smoke House. Fruits, vegetables, and a variety of flowers are still grown on the plantation.

Boone Hall Plantation

Cape Hatteras National Seashore

The Cape Hatteras Lighthouse beckons visitors to more than 70 miles of shoreline along the outer banks of North Carolina. Once there, fishing, boating, swimming, surfing, bird watching, and many other activities await. The area earned the nickname "Graveyard of the Atlantic" because of its dangerous currents, reefs, and storms.

A cooper and his helpers make churns, tubs, and barrels out of wood.

Colonial Williamsburg

The world's largest living history museum is found in Williamsburg, Virginia. Visiting "colonists" can sample colonial foods, tour restored historic buildings, watch demonstrations, and meet people who dress and speak like 18th-century colonists.

Harpers Ferry National Historical Park

Harpers Ferry, West Virginia, has been the site of many important historical events. The town was a key weapons-manufacturing site, an early railroad junction, and a Civil War battle zone. In 1859, **abolitionist** John Brown and a small band of men raided the Federal Armory in Harpers Ferry to steal guns for slaves. Brown hoped to help slaves fight for their freedom. Instead he was caught and hanged for **treason**. His raid, however, did bring attention to the issue of slavery, and the Civil War began a year and a half later.

Harpers Ferry

Orleans, Louisiana, introduce tourists to the mysterious beauty of the swamp. Cypress trees and other unusual swamp plants surround the waterways. Guides point out alligators, black bear, deer, fish, and exotic birds.

Honey Island got its name from the honey bees once spotted in the area.

Homosassa Springs State Wildlife Park

Homosassa Springs State Wildlife Park, north of Tampa, Florida, is a wildlife refuge for West Indian manatees. From an underwater observatory, visitors can watch these endangered mammals swim and feed in the spring waters of the Homosassa River. A stroll on the boardwalk that runs through the park features other wildlife, such as bobcats, cougars, otters, bears, and birds.

Honey Island Swamp

Boat tours through Honey Island Swamp near New

Jekyll Island

Where can you find miles of beach, four golf courses, a water park, several bike paths, and an award-winning tennis center? On Jekyll Island, a barrier island off the coast of Georgia. Once a resort for American millionaires, Jekyll Island is now a popular vacation spot for people from all walks of life.

Mineral formations in Mammoth Cave

Mammoth Cave National Park

Mammoth Cave National Park near Bowling Green, Kentucky, contains more than 360 miles of underground caves.

It is the longest recorded cave system in the world. Rangers guide tours and explain the beautiful mineral formations in the caves.

The Ozark Folk Center

The Ozark Folk Center near Mountain View, Arkansas, shares the heritage of the Ozark Mountain people through exhibits, crafts, and handmade goods. The music theater presents regular performances of mountain music.

U.S. Space and Rocket Center

The U.S. Space and Rocket Center in Huntsville, Alabama, displays rockets and other spacecraft. Hands-on activities and demonstrations teach about the past, present, and future of space flight and exploration. Rides on the Space Shot and G-Force Accelerator make the journey to space come alive.

A full-scale exhibit of the Pathfinder space shuttle is on display at the U.S. Space and Rocket Center.

Vicksburg National Military Park

During the Civil War, Union troops and ships surrounded and shelled Vicksburg, Mississippi, for 47 days. They fought to gain control of the Mississippi River. Food became scarce, and several townspeople lived in **trenches** and caves. Many of the remains of this battle have been preserved at the Vicksburg National Military Park.

Chapter 6

Famous Faces from the Southeast

Every U.S. region can boast of special people who have made important contributions to the world. These are a few of the famous faces from the Southeast.

Muhammad Ali (1942–present)

Born in Louisville, Kentucky, Muhammad Ali was the world's heavyweight boxing champion from 1964 to 1967. When asked to describe his fighting style, Ali said, "I float like a butterfly and sting like a bee."

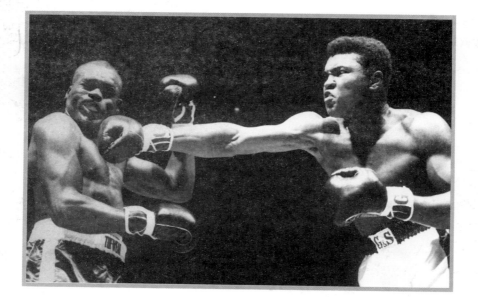

Louis Armstrong
(1901–1971)

Like many jazz musicians, Louis Armstrong grew up in New Orleans, Louisiana. He played the trumpet, sang, and appeared in movies. Armstrong's talent, style, and personality made him the "father of jazz."

Sing a Song of the South

Several types of music have their roots in the Southeast. Gospel and blues music came from the songs of slaves. Jazz also started among African Americans in the late 19th century. Bluegrass is a southern style of music played on fiddles, banjos, guitars, and mandolins.

George Washington Carver (1864?–1943)

Born a slave, George Washington Carver became a scientist, a researcher, a teacher, and an inventor. He taught at the Tuskegee Institute in Alabama for 47 years. Carter greatly influenced agriculture in the

Southeast by finding hundreds of uses for crops such as peanuts, sweet potatoes, and pecans.

Gloria Estefan
(1957–present)

This pop singer was just a toddler when her family left Cuba and moved to Miami, Florida. In her early 20s, Gloria Estefan joined a Latin band and quickly became the lead singer. Since then, she has continued to top the charts and tour the world, entertaining fans with her unique blend of Latin American and pop music.

Francis Marion
(1732?–1795)

During the American Revolution, Francis Marion was known as the "Swamp Fox." He and his small band of soldiers were very successful at causing trouble for British soldiers and then disappearing into the South Carolina swamps.

Edgar Allan Poe
(1809–1849)

Raised in Richmond, Virginia, Edgar Allan Poe became a famous author known for his poetry and frightening short stories. The Poe Museum in Richmond honors Poe's contributions to literature.

Elvis Presley
(1935–1977)

The "King of Rock and Roll" was born in Tupelo, Mississippi. Elvis Presley thrilled audiences with his bold style of rock and roll music. He also starred in more than 30 movies. Thousands of people visit Graceland, his mansion in Tennessee, every year.

Mary Lou Retton
(1968–present)

Mary Lou Retton was the first American to win an Olympic gold medal in the All-Around gymnastics competition. In 1984, this native of Fairmont, West Virginia, scored perfect 10s on the vault and floor exercise to push her to the top spot. She also won four other medals that year. Today, she is a sportscaster and motivational speaker.

Jackie Robinson
(1919–1972)

Born in Cairo, Georgia, Jackie Robinson became the first African American to play major league baseball. In 1947, Robinson joined the Brooklyn Dodgers. He withstood years of segregation, threats, and name calling to open the doors for all African American men who wanted to play major league baseball.

Sam Walton
(1918–1992)

Sam Walton opened his first Wal-Mart store in Rogers, Arkansas, in 1962. He bought large quantities of products at a discount, so he could sell items at lower prices than other stores. Wal-Mart has since become the nation's largest **retailer**.

http://en.wikipedia.org/wiki/U.S._Southern_states
Explore the southeastern region of the United States with this overview of its geography, culture, history, and economy.

http://infoplease.com/states.html
Choose a state from the Southeast region and view a map and state profile. Includes basic statistics, state symbols, and famous faces.

http://www.factmonster.com/ipka/A0875011.html
Learn "monstrous" facts about the southern area of the United States.

http://www.50states.com/bio/
Click on each of the states in the Southeast to find a list and brief description of the many famous faces from the region.

To visit the 12 states of the Southeast region, tour these official state Web sites.

http://www.state.al.us/ (Alabama)
http://www.state.ar.us/ (Arkansas)
http://www.myflorida.com/ (Florida)
http://www.georgia.gov/ (Georgia)
http://kentucky.gov/ (Kentucky)
http://www.louisiana.gov/wps/portal/ (Louisiana)
http://www.state.ms.us/index.jsp (Mississippi)
http://www.ncgov.com/ (North Carolina)
http://www.myscgov.com/ (South Carolina)
http://www.state.tn.us/ (Tennessee)
http://www.virginia.gov/cmsportal/ (Virginia)
http://www.wv.gov/ (West Virginia)

America's Civil War by L. L. Owens. What was life like before the Civil War? Why did the war begin? How did it end? This book answers these and other questions. Perfection Learning Corporation, 2000. [RL 3.5 IL 2–6] (5968601 PB 5968602 CC)

The Civil War by Shirley Jordan. From the election of Abraham Lincoln to the abolition of slavery, the United States nearly destroyed itself from within. Perfection Learning Corporation, 1999. [RL 3.6   IL 4–9] (5669802 PB 5669802 CC)

Free to Learn by Thomas S. Owens. Everyone is happy with Mrs. Blackwell's Dame School until she accepts a freed slave as a student. Perfection Learning Corporation, 2000. [RL 2   IL 2–6] (5904701 PB 5904702 CC)

The Long Journey to Freedom by Susan Grohmann. In 1815, a family escapes slavery in Florida. Three years later, they are caught up in the First Seminole War. Perfection Learning Corporation, 2002. [RL 3.1 IL 4–8] (3856501 PB 3856502 CC)

George Washington Carver by Andy Carter and Carole Saller. This book recounts the life of the African American agriculturist at the Tuskegee Institute, emphasizing his love of plants and his belief in living in harmony with the natural world. Lerner, 2001. [RL 2 IL 2–6] (3435701 PB 3435706 HB)

The Trail of Tears: An American Tragedy by Tracy Barrett. On May 10, 1838, the Cherokee still living in Georgia were forced to leave their homes and take a long, dangerous journey. Perfection Learning Corporation, 2000. [RL 5 IL 2–6] (5902401 PB 5902402 CC)

What If You'd Been at Jamestown? by Ellen Keller. A colonist experiences the settling of Jamestown—from sailing the Atlantic to the starving time. Perfection Learning Corporation, 1997. [RL 1.8 IL 2–6] (4982301 PB 4982302 CC)

•RL = Reading Level
•IL = Interest Level
Perfection Learning's catalog numbers are included for your ordering convenience. PB indicates paperback. CC indicates Cover Craft. HB indicates hardback.

Glossary

abolitionist
(ab uh LISH uh nist) person who worked to end slavery

alluvial plain
(uh LOOV ee uhl playn) area of flat land where sand and soil from a river are deposited

aquaculture
(AHK wah kuhl cher) farming of sea animals for profit

assassinated
(uh SAS uh nay ted) killed by a sudden violent attack; usually refers to well-known people

barge (barj) long, narrow flat-bottomed boat used for transporting goods

barrier island
(BAIR ee er EYE land) long sandy island that runs along a coastline and protects the shore from erosion (see separate entry for *erosion*)

colonist (KAH luh nist) person who settled in North America before it became the United States

dam (dam) barrier of dirt or concrete built across a river to control the flow of water

decaying (dee KAY ing) breaking down; rotting

deposit (dee PAH zit) amount or quantity of material found in one spot

descendant (dee SEN dent) relative of people who came before

economy (ee KON uh mee) region's system of making, buying, and selling goods and services

erosion (uh ROH zhuhn) wearing away of soil by wind and water

fertile (FER tuhl) good for growing

hospitality (hah spit TAL i tee) friendly welcome or treatment

immigrant (IM uh gruhnt) person who moves to one country from another country

indigo (IN di goh) plant used to make blue dye

integrate (IN tuh grayt) to open to all people, regardless of race

merchant (MER chent) related to the selling of products; type of boat used for such purposes

mound (mownd) hill of dirt where the dead are buried

natural resource
(NATCH er uhl REE sors)
material, such as coal or wood,
that is found in nature

New World (noo wurld) land
now called North and South
America

peat (peet) tightly packed
deposits of once-living things that
have decomposed or rotted (see
separate entry for *deposit*)

plain (playn) large area of flat
land, usually with few trees

plateau (plat OH) hill or
mountain with a flat top

precipitation
(pree sip uh TAY shuhn)
moisture that falls from the
clouds, such as rain and snow

receded (ri SEE ded) moved
back or away; withdrew

reform (ree FORM) to change
or improve something

retailer (REE tail er) store that
sells goods to customers

revolt (ree VOLT) to protest or
take action against rules and
authority

rural (ROOR uhl) having to do
with life in the country

segregation
(seg ruh GAY shuhn) separation
or division between groups of
people, especially due to race

sharecropper (SHAIR krahp er)
worker who farms land for an
owner and is paid a share of the
profits

silt (silt) mud, sand, and soil
carried by a river

spring (spring) water that flows
out of the ground and forms a
small stream or pool

subtropical
(sub TRAH pik uhl) having hot,
humid weather for much of the
year

textile (TEKS teyel) woven
fabric; cloth

treason (TREE zuhn) crimes
against one's own country

trench (trench) long, deep hole
dug in the ground used for
defense against enemy fire

urban (ER bin) having to do
with life in the city

wetland (WET land) area of
land with very moist soil due to
complete or partial coverage by
water

Index